Srdjan Jo
with a series of pho

SOCIALIST ARCHITECTURE

—

THE REAPPEARING ACT

THE
GREENBOX

SOCIALIST ARCHITECTURE
THE REAPPEARING ACT

"... decentralized planning is the extremely significant factor in the economic efficiency of planning particularly in a self-managed and democratic planning system. Without a certain degree of decentralization, the planning system would become the tool in the hands of the state."[1]
Edvard Kardelj

This book presents experiences of exploring decentralized socialist architecture across Yugoslavia between 2006 and 2011. Like on a safari, Armin Linke and I found these sites appearing as spatial creatures that we believe were not in the intended official view. At times we played ball in empty halls spontaneously with curious kids who were around. At times we had to ward off angry people (and stray dogs and birds) who saw us gathering documentation. Yet, we were in a position to immerse into the success of the architecture of socialist cause. These places that had been made in the name of global inclusion of Yugoslavia's soft socialism, today perform the reappearing act of their own success and spatial magic. These locations are now emptied of the ideology that made them. On the other hand, they are full of a new kind of life, and today this significance is more open-ended than ever intended.

1   Kardelj, Edvard, *The System of Planning in a Society of Self-management: Brioni Discussions*, Belgrade: Socialist Thought and Practice, 1976, 12, Note: Kardelj was the chief ideologue of socialist Yugoslavia.

The Socialist Federation of the Republic of Yugoslavia vanished during the early 1990s. It was *Balkanized* into a number of emerging democracies and former socialist states. Each of these former Yugoslav states inherited monuments, buildings, landscapes, and infrastructures, which were constructed specifically for Yugoslav soft socialist postures and representations. After Yugoslavia vanished, most of the inherited institutional architecture was left vacant and in a state of limbo between repurpose and reuse, or continuing as modern archaeological ruins. The *Reappearing Act* book interprets the quandary facing a few emerging democracies today: Croatia, Macedonia, Montenegro and Serbia, that came out of Yugoslavia among other new states. The effects of the lack of a decisive outcome for their abandonded socialist architecture creates the spatial experience and the fate of historical Yugoslav architecture – as a form of success.

Like a magic trick, the vanishing act constitutes the re-appearance of things that have been lost from other forms and other mediums. For traditional architecture, which is materially and spatially bound to its own body, organization and loci, vanishing appears as a particular and destructive process of removal and dismantling. However, for architecture tailored to socialism, the disappearance of the very ideology that constructed it can put into question the traditional relation between body, form, and social and political intentions in architecture. Instead of claiming that the vanishing of an idea causes the non-negotiable material appearance of the neglect of the past, what could be proposed is that the vanishing act of socialism leaves this ideology in the past as such. Thus the vanishing act pushes the remaining socialist architecture towards the future. What has vanished always reappears in unexpected forms that surprise us.

In the time of transition after socialism the archaeology of architecture from socialist Yugoslavia got differentiated in terms of public memory. *The Vanishing Act* shows that the memorials of the former socialist regime in Yugoslavia are mostly located in the countryside in between these new capitals. The countryside that these memorials occupy are in a liminal space in between seats of political power. We have also demonstrated a connection between the materialization of *Balkanization* to the concept of *timeliness* coming from the discourse on the *imaginary* by Maria Todorova. This was done in an attempt to ground the idea of the imaginary and its subsequent discourse of the metaphorical *Balkanization* into a material terrain where we trace a concept we have termed the *architecture of Balkanization*. By traversing eight contemporary capital cities of former Yugoslavia we see how Todorova's concept of *timeliness* operates across multiple and overlapping territories with various stages of the *architecture of Balkanization* occurring simultaneously. From its rendition as autonomous zones in Ljubljana, via self-regulated urbanism in Serbia and Macedonia, climatic architecture in Tirana to an anti-climax in Sarajevo, each producing a specific, distinct type of spatial practice, on the *architecture of Balkanization*.

The traditional perception of socialism as a unified, centralized political system can be misleading in observing socialist Yugoslavia as a uniform territory. The prior political arrangement of the territory, unified in socialist-extrovert Yugoslavia and socialist-introvert Albania, held looser control over the uniform expression in architecture. Furthermore, we may be misled too easily if we accept that the fall of Yugoslavia was a severing of socialist uniformity from democratic pluralism. The thesis in this book is that due to the particularly *softer* version of socialism in the former Yugoslavia under Josip Broz Tito, the uniformity of representation in architecture did not actually exist, nor was it imposed as a political program. Yugoslavia's political mechanism did go to great lengths to maintain the particularity of its constitutional parts. In order do so, the politics of engaging spatial practices were designed on a rotational basis between Yugoslav republics and Autonomous Provinces. Thus, the fall of Yugoslavia did not break the continuity of the ethnic-state particularity of spatial practices. Instead, the *Balkanization* of Yugoslavia *in-situ* enabled into multiple new countries and capital cities added a higher degree of national particularity. The national particularities were superimposed over Yugoslavia's internal distinctions in the period of late socialism. This work explores a series of memorials, monuments, and political institutions such as the museums or homes of the revolution as they are today – mostly empty. The reason for looking at this architecture is not to comment on their state of being defunct, but to examine the plurality of architectural approaches to memory and representation of socialism, and juxtapose the diversity of these approaches to that of the unregulated construction in the emerging democracies.

The recent geopolitical change in favor of nationalism is practiced in the distinction of emerging capital cities coming out of Yugoslavia and its own self-*Balkanization* process. In the past there was one capital city of Yugoslavia: Belgrade, and now there are six more: Ljubljana, Podgorica, Prishtina, Sarajevo, Skopje and Zagreb (in the alphabetical order). This makes *Balkanization* a successful producer of capital cities, at a rate of 600% increase of capital-ness. The Vanishing Act, like in the magician Houdini's performance, is not about disappearance, but about re-appearance in unexpected ways.

Once it vanished, Yugoslav socialism left scores of architecture seemingly behind. That architecture, tailored to the particular characteristics of Yugoslav socialism, is now mostly abandoned and in disrepair, but more public than they ever intended to be. The best examples of this destiny are the two institution buildings left alone in the birthplace of Josip Broz Tito in Kumrovec, Croatia: The *Former Yugoslav Memorial Home* and the *Political School.* Both built as part of a socialist political resort in the years between 1974 and 1981, the structures stand open, neglected, and for sale. They were built as part of the state-wide initiative to find a suitable location for the education of aspiring politicians in the former Yugoslavia. The 1970s and 1980s were crisis years in Yugoslav socialism. The economy was in decline, Tito was approaching old age. Latent nationalist forces, which Tito had kept at a distance, were regrouping. Yet the commissions for the politically motivated architecture went forward. The *Yugoslav Memorial Home* was built in 1974, the *Political School* in 1981. The site is surrounded by the varied topography where Josip Broz Tito was born and where he spent the early part of his life.

The resort's design scheme, conceived by two Croatian architects, won a 1972 competition in Kumrovec for a Socialist version of a political retreat. Its political nature lies in the change from the typical socialist modernist style based on a North American expressionless corporate model towards a more expressive style inspired by Scandinavian and Finnish sources. By the 1970s young Slovenian architects were already adopting this trend in their statist architecture and design. The institutional buildings in Ljubljana such as the *Cankarjev Dom* as well as the highly expressive *House of the Opera and Ballet* in Skopje, Macedonia, both by 1970s Slovenian architects, were all inspired by the mountainous geometrics, peaks and morphologies of the more rural areas of Alpine Slovenia. Croatian architecture of the 1950s and 1960s was based on a restrained and stark post-war modernism. The fact that the village of Kumrovec lies on the Croatian border of Slovenia may be the main reason why the architects Berislav Šerbetić and Ivan Filipčić departed from the dominant direction of their state to adopt a more rural expression for the *Yugoslav Memorial Home*'s largely modern complex. Indeed, the model of identity may be analogous to Tito's border identity, himself a Slovenian who grew up just across the border in Croatia.

Yugoslav Memorial Home, Kumrovec, Croatia,
Architects: Berislav Šerbetić & Ivan Filipčić, built 1974,
photographed in 2010

The architecture of the *Yugoslav Memorial Home* follows the model of civic design in the deep countryside originated by the Finnish architect Alvar Aalto in the aftermath of World War II. Instead of a single rectangular volume largely associated with urban socialist modernism, this countryside model is based on a landscape approach. The memorial home is essentially an artificial plinth designed as a smooth and invisible transition to the hilltop where stand two opposing volumes with social and residential use. The space between them, the top of the "hill" is meant to be the open and protected social space that we could call a "square in the countryside". The space below the square connects the two buildings into a single interior complex. Thus the entire composition blends half into the landscape, concealing its true size. The logic of fragmentation continues into the interior by the use of multiple platform levels each of which is intended for different uses such as lobby, cafe, lounge, banquet and pool, connected in a sequence by stairs and sight. The use of wood and soft floor surfaces punctuated by the arrays of structural wooden beams as well as hanging brown tinted globe glass lamps all evoke the atmosphere of a modern cottage. This expression of interchangeability of dense urbanity stranded in deep countryside foregrounds the current period of intended exchangeability between ethnic and urban-rural classes. The exchangeability of both is in no way ethnic, nor national itself, which was a key praxis of Tito's to further amalgamate multiple ethnicities together in a socialist system. This ideology vanished, and the buildings stand open, exposed to the encroaching flora and fauna. They are also more *public* then was ever intended to be so.

The pragmatics of Yugoslav *soft* socialism gives foundations to such friendly-yet-authoritative architecture vis-à-vis ideology. Edvard Kardelj, the "chief architect of socialist Yugoslavia", is often quoted with his maxim from 1953 that "discrimination is impossible according to the very foundations of the socialist system".[2] Edvard Kardelj was a young Slovenian teacher when he met Tito in prison. We can see Kardelj and his teachings as a political prelude to the spatial practices as well, that no discrimination should be made possible in socialist architecture (and art) either. The impossibility of discrimination should be carried forward in socialist versions of architecture and urbanism. The *interchangeable* process of design thus must not derive from any ethnic nor national sources because one would surely project itself over the other. The architects who complied with the *interchangeable* incentive looked for references elsewhere in the world (avoiding the array of centralist socialist countries like the Soviet Union) to supplant the taboo of a local and ethnic source.

Kardelj repeatedly championed not only the importance, but the "extreme significance" of decentralized planning in order to diminish the powers of the state. For example, one of the main citations from Kardelj reads: "… decentralized planning is the extremely significant factor in the economic efficiency of planning particularly in a self-managed and democratic planning system. Without a certain degree of decentralization, the planning system would become the tool in the hands of the state."[3] In a

2   Audrey Helfant Budding's chapter in Cohen, Lenard J., and Jasna Dragović-Soso (eds.), *State Collapse in South-Eastern Europe: New Perspectives on Yugoslavia's Disintegration,* West Lafayette, IN: Purdue UP, 2008, 107. This footnote has been borrowed from Đinđić, Zoran, *Jugoslavija kao nedovršena država,* 28. Cf. Slobodan Samardžić, "Federalizm u Švajcarskoj i Jugoslaviji – ustavni koncepti u političke institucije," in Thomas Flajner and Slobodan Samardžić (eds.), *Federalizam i problem manjina u višeetničkim zajednicama – uporedna analiza Švajcarske i Jugoslavije,* Belgrade: Institut za evropske studije, 1995, 37.

3   Kardelj, Edvard, *The System of Planning in a Society of Self-management: Brioni Discussions,* Belgrade: Socialist Thought and Practice, 1976, 12.

process of Yugoslavia's first deploying the American corporate model as the representation of the post World War II state, then switching to the Scandinavian organic model, Kardelj's idea of architecture kept Yugoslav post-war design efforts pragmatic, neutralizing, and non-original. If we are even more lucid with the interpretation of this political direction, we can say that the result of the socialist non-discriminative axiom is that Yugoslav architecture was steered towards a non-national practice. This emerging non-national socialist practice was performed by individuals, trained professionals with an array of multiply declared ethnicities never actually reaching a common core.[4] In fact, the non-nationalism was explained as Yugoslav socialist patriotism, which is "not the opposite of but rather a necessary internationalist supplement to democratic national consciousness, in the conditions of the socialist community of nations."[5]

The second building in Kumrovec, the *Political School*, was allegedly commissioned by Tito himself and was built at a later date in 1981. Tito died in 1980. However, based on the complex Yugoslav system of ethnic integration, ensuing design commissions were assigned by a rotational principle of offering jobs to architects based on their home state republic. This was called the "key" rotational concept. The "key" concept was the result of Yugoslavia's late socialist process of decentralization and gradual equation of distinct ethnicities with distinct states *(deetatizacija)*. We shall describe this process after mentioning that as the result of the rotational "key" principle of strategic positions representing

4   A summary of the flight and decline of the project to institute the Yugoslav ethnicity with multiple sources quoted can be found in: Audrey Helfant Budding's chapter in Cohen, Lenard J., and Jasna Dragović-Soso (eds.), *State Collapse in South-Eastern Europe: New Perspectives on Yugoslavia's Disintegration*, West Lafayette, IN: Purdue UP, 2008, 101.

5   Ibid, 101, citing the 1958 League of Communist of Yugoslavia Program *(Program Saveza komunista Jugoslavije)*, 147–148.

complex system of Yugoslavia, the authorship of the *Political School* is still unresolved. The vanishing authorship gave way to the current use of the buildings as free playgrounds for children, incidental visitors and tourists. As a result, the resort today is more publicly accessible than was ever intended.

The building of the *Political School* itself is a single bar, tilted on the side to respond to the hilly landscape across the site. As opposed to the *Yugoslav Memorial Home,* which incorporates a publicly accessible square on its own roof, the *Political School* does this by close proximity to a steep hill. The main entrance and the open auditorium is thus placed in between the back of the building and the hill, a space of about 20 meters wide. The steep, inclined volume of the *Political School* acts as a "mask" to the hill behind, and an offset of the hill's own sectional geometry. Inside, due to its bar typology, the organization is largely linear with lengths of corridor that make the linearity seemingly without center. Though there is a central space identified as the social area and a bar, no special material treatment of the interior was deployed to differentiate it from the very last room in the complex.

Here we need to describe the *rotational key* system in socialist politics and its impact on spatial socialist practices such as architecture, primarily as the centripetal force in the *architecture of Balkanization.* Between the construction of the *Yugoslav Memorial Home* built between 1972 and 1974, and the completion of the second building, the *Political School,* in 1981, the Yugoslav constitution went through rapid, dramatic changes on paper and in practice. The biggest and most profound change from the era of "non-discriminative socialism" of the 1950s and 1960s, was the appearance of the gap between the personal nationality and state ethnicity. Tito introduced Yugoslav nationality as a personal choice in an attempt to blur the multi-ethnic composition of

Political School, Kumrovec, Croatia,
Architects: Berislav Šerbetić, Ivan Filipčić, built 1981,
photographed in 2010

Yugoslavia. However this project for the common national identity was not followed through and the "Yugoslav" nation never reached a true legal status. A person who declared himself or herself a "Yugoslav" on the census or elsewhere was "not stating a national identity but rather exercising the right not to declare one", citing the controversial Croatian communist Stipe Šuvar most involved in the national question in socialist Yugoslavia.[6] The alliance of multiple nationalities introduced by Tito was gradually elevated to the idea of *Yugoslavism* by Kardelj exactly at the time of the planning of the Kumrovec *Yugoslav Memorial Home,* yet *Yugoslavism* received silent resistance as an utopian idea.[7] Kardelj, the main author behind Yugoslav constitutions had to amend it. He did it by accepting to equate the personal ethnic identity and the state collective identity into a single strategic position, thus allowing for ethnic self-determination to become national. The idea of *Yugoslavism* was fragmented, and *proto Balkanized,* with the release of the constitution of 1974 sealing the failure of the personal determination as a Yugoslav.[8] The 1974 constitution of Yugoslavia, which remained in effect through the end of the 1980s, only partially reversed the extreme decentralization of the early 1970s. With 406 original articles, it was one of the longest constitutions in the world. It added

6 Ibid, 120.

7 Ibid, 120, footnotes cite the work of Dejan Jović, "Yugoslavism and Yugoslav Communism: from Tito to Kardelj", in Dejan Djokić (ed.), *Yugoslavism: History of a Failed Idea* 1918–1992, London, Hurst & Company, 157–181. Here we have to note that anyone who would challenge the idea of Kardelj of the seemless Yugoslavism, such as Tito did himself, would be labeled a "unitarist".

8 Jovanovic Weiss, Srdjan, "Toward a Positive Balkanization," *Via Occupation,* Morgan Martinson (ed.), Philadelphia, PA: PDSP/School of Design, University of Pennsylvania, 2008, 74–77.

elaborate language protecting the self-management system from state interference and expanding representation of republics and provinces in all electoral and policy forums. The Constitution called the restructured Federal Assembly the highest expression of the self-management system. In order to keep the democratic allocation of commissions the "key" system was introduced, where each state nation (from each republic) would get a strategic position at an order previously established by consensus. This rotational practice dramatically influenced architecture, urbanism, and spatial planning as architects from distinct republics could get commissioned in any other republic simply because of the rotational "key". Yet the "key" did nothing to prevent the rising dissatisfaction of national architects who did not like to see other national architects building in their front yard.

As a result, the *Political School* in Kumrovec has no definitive authors. If the authorship is known, it is neglected due to the "key" system's limitation in capturing the emotional collective space attempted by *Yugoslavism*. However, due to the increasing *Balkanization* between the republic states of Yugoslavia and the rise of the republic national interest, the authors from another state may have been neglected simply because other priorities arose to emotionally carve out a sense of national territory and belonging. According to Marko Sančanin, director of Platforma 9.81 based in Zagreb, a young team from Belgrade, Serbia won the design competition for the *Political School* in Kumrovec. Ironically, the authorship for both Croatian architects Šerbetić and Filipčić lacked national approval as the two steered away from a "nationally" recognizable architecture and adopted a shared Yugoslav direction towards non-nationality of built places by importing the Scandinavian model of architecture.

After the gradual vanishing of Yugoslavia, and with the political independence of Croatia, both these structures in Kumrovec have become obsolete and were vacated, though not immediately.

The buildings were used to temporarily house the refugees from the raging war in Slavonia, the North Eastern part of the country with cities under siege such as Vukovar. The conflict was initiated by Slobodan Milošević, who dispatched the Yugoslav People's Army (JNA) and its paramilitaries in the attempt to seize power within a territory associated closely with this unresolved emotional collective space. Paradoxically, most of the refugees fleeing Vukovar and Slavonia were housed in buildings in Kumrovec that represented socialist Yugoslavia while its army chased them away from their homes.

Even though Tito was an avant-garde communist, the plaque that stands outside his childhood home reads: "His failure is that he lost what he had made". This statement comes as an acute expression of a widespread disdain towards Tito departing without securing viable plans for the future of socialism. Yugoslav socialism vanished soon after Tito's death in 1980 – one year before the completion of the *Political School* in 1981 – leaving behind unresolved social problems as well as the deep disappointment in the perceived failure of a local hero.

Today, these two remarkable buildings in Kumrovec are in a state of neglect. Yet the neglect seems to be working towards their unintended qualities which no one could perceive nor plan for. The Croatian government has tried to sell the structures without much success. The usual reason for the unsuccessful transaction quotes the high level of non-adaptability of the buildings' layouts and materials for contemporary uses, such as a hotel, resort or an educational facility, as prescribed by the bid posted by the Croatian government. On the other hand, the remarkable lack of flexibility or elasticity of the two buildings' organization, layout, and form keeps them in a preserved form touched only by natural elements and some looting. Furthermore, these buildings are becoming more like the nature they were mimicking in their original design expressions. As the flora and fauna take over both the *Yugoslav Memorial Home* and the *Political School,* their resistance to transition into emerging capitalism marks them as socialist ruins. At the same time, they have never been as publicly accessible as they are now. The most organic approach would be to use them as places that can absorb neglect as the quality of their own future vis-à-vis the vanishing act of Yugoslav socialism. What re-appears after the vanishing act of socialism is local nature, with its adaptable flora and fauna, without a center or periphery, like an oversized stone in an ideological garden.

Kardelj's *Yugoslavism* and decentralization policies resulted in the 1974 constitution and in the "key" system of rotation. The architects working for the socialist system could now count on using their expertise all across the country. However, the system stipulated that they could only do it only once in six years in one of the six officially recognized republic states: Slovenia, Serbia, Croatia, Montenegro, Macedonia and Bosnia & Herzegovina. To by-pass the "key" system of limiting architects from a certain republic to one commission in six years, the architects from the individual republic states developed expert design solutions for distinct typologies of architecture needed across the country. Strategically, they could offer expert design to the other five states around the six year clock of the "key" system. Even though the 1974 Constitution of Yugoslavia recognized two autonomous provinces within Serbia: Vojvodina and Kosovo, those two were still under the umbrella of Serbia when the *rotational key* system was adopted. However, both provinces could exercise their own commissions on their own territories and even commission foreign architects to design key state institutions. The best example is the massive *Serbian National Theatre* in Novi Sad, commissioned to a Polish architect and executed by local architectural firms in the 1980s. In each state, architects picked a specialization: Slovenian architects developed the typology of cultural centers, theaters and opera halls; Croatian architects became experts in museums

for the state as well as hotels for the Adriatic coast; Serbian architects largely developed mass housing for civilian and military use,
as well as department stores; Bosnian architects became experts
in preservation and sports, recreational and cultural typologies.
Macedonian architects had to wait for the earthquake of 1963 in
order to adopt the influence of Kenzo Tange's brutalist aesthetics
as he delivered his master plan for the reconstruction of Skopje.
Thus, in theory, all six distinct republics could rotate their expertise in distinct typologies around socialist Yugoslavia without
discrimination, as Kardelj's socialist mantra would suggest. Due
to their narrow focus on developing specific ideologies, architects
began to exhibit a diverse and distinct set of styles. Slovenian
architects developed an organic, landscape-based approach to
cultural institutions, Croatian architects developed stark modernist box-like architecture with a combination of concrete and
glass, Serbian architects developed slab architecture, long or
short or towers as the main expression of mass housing, and
Macedonian architects took on the brutalist aesthetics for almost
every institution built after the earthquake of 1963. It is Bosnian
architects who managed to work with more than a few typologies, due to their central position in Yugoslavia and the local mix
of ethnicities. They worked with everything from contemporary
interpretations of Islamic architecture to the expressive structures of sport and convention centers.

The praxis showed that these typological and aesthetic divisions
were exceptions to the national rule during the *rotational key*
system among the republic states. Montenegro, for example did
not have a school of architecture like the other republics at the
time. It sent students to other universities around Yugoslavia and,
in return, they engaged prominent architects from each of the
other centers in the former Yugoslavia in Montenegro allowing
for strong influences, and were in a way free to mix typologies

The Home of the Revolution, Nikšić, Montenegro,
Architect: Marko Mušič, building unfinished,
photographed in 2010

and styles of work. Here also lies the key to the continuity of architecture from socialism to early capitalism in the former Yugoslavia: the quality of distinct republics has been mobilized and dispatched to the others. There a sort of a prototypical *Balkanization* starts to take place on a strategic level of political urban planning and transfer of architectural knowledge.

The most extraordinary example is the architecture of the *Home of the Revolution* in the city of Nikšić in Montenegro, by the Slovenian architect and academic Marko Mušič. Revolution-themed museums in Serbia were designed by Croatian architects. Some of those are complete and in use like the *Museum of Revolution* in Novi Sad and some are left incomplete and abandoned like the *Museum of Revolution* in Belgrade by the Croatian architect Vjenceslav Richter. Awarding the commission to an emerging Slovenian architect (who specialized in organic and landscape-inspired architecture) was a breakthrough in Yugoslavia's complex politics of decentralized architecture commissions. The decision represented a move beyond the increasingly bureaucratized allocation of commissions to architects who specialize in specific building typologies. Indeed, Kardelj disagreed with specialization, arguing that it would lead to ethnicity-based monopolies. Whenever Kardelj sensed that ethnic architects were specializing in specific building typologies, he adjusted the rules to undermine the specialization. This maneuvering in internal politics of decentralization culminated in the 1974 Yugoslavian constitution which codified the *rotational key* system.

The logic behind Kardelj's decentralization of practice was theoretically clear – it sought to disperse technology across the multi-ethnic and highly discrepant territory of the former Yugoslavia in terms of education and skills. This *idealistic* policy of mandated rotation is surprising in a country in which the teachings of Marx's dialectical materialism were part of the regular curriculum in middle and high schools in

Yugoslavia. Not surprisingly, the policy of idealistic *rotational key* was met with significant disdain, especially from the less developed republics in the former Yugoslavia who often lost jobs to more developed states. Officially, the republics accepted projects made according to the *rotational key*. However, they went through the process without much enthusiasm for sharing work with other architects. Tito's Yugoslav socialism "glue", which largely depended on popular enthusiasm about the common goal of victory over fascism, was wearing off. As enthusiasm waned, the emotional "glue" was being replaced with the political glue of the rotating key policy. The construction of the *Home of the Revolution* started in 1979. By 1980, the year of Tito's death, the focus shifted to the aftermath of political succession. A single pragmatic leader was to be supplanted by the use of the *rotational key* system. The presidency would now rotate on a yearly basis among the six republics. The rotational presidency created a discontinuity in federal projects and initiatives, and gradually eroded relations between the republics. Later *Balkanization* was initiated within the late socialist system with Kardelj's constitution of 1974. "As far as architecture and architects were concerned, the late 1960s and early 1970s were a golden age, brimming with public competitions and frequently awarded projects."[9]

Following Tito's death, the *Home of the Revolution* in Nikšić was at first postponed, then left incomplete. As the socialist system gradually vanished in the year 1991 and with the beginning of the short war between Yugoslavia and a seceding Slovenia, the *Home of the Revolution* would have been all but forgotten, were it not for its immense scale and high visibility in the very center

9   Krečič, Peter, "Architecture in Former Yugoslavia," Dubravka Djurić and Miško Šuvaković (eds.), *Impossible Histories: Historical Avant-gardes, Neo-avant-gardes, and Post-avant-gardes in Yugoslavia, 1918–1991,* Cambridge, MA: MIT, 2006, 360.

of the Nikšić city center. The structure became an unintended, unattended and unprotected piece of socialist archaeology. According to news media in Montenegro, about 14 deaths have been recorded since the abandonment of the location. The last two deaths were reported in 2011.[10]

The *reappearing idea of socialist revolution* has re-emerged here in the form of interior gardens and an informal economy. The *Home of the Revolution* in Nikšić lives by the forces of the future of neglect. The pop-up gardens, small lakes and fauna that encroach onto the large house only accentuate the new natural revolution in the science of natural urban systems. The content of the revolution has been replaced by small yet typical and repetitive icons of the micro-economy: kiosks built in masonry flanking the empty *Home of the Revolution.* What has vanished as content (the collective revolution) reappears as cubicles of democratic transfiguration of individuality. Some scholars of the history of Yugoslav socialism see its architecture as part of an unfinished modernization. I would like to suggest that the architecture in question is actually independent from the ideology of modernization, and that the ideology itself is instead incomplete. Even though the government has been discussing options to either remove or renovate the *Home of the Revolution,* the cost of both means that not much will be done in the years to come.[11] The architecture of distinction here relied on the dislocation of high-tech knowledge from Slovenia to Montenegro, from the most advanced republic to one of the least developed republics in the

10 Kadić, V. "Nikšić: Dve Nove žrtve Doma Revolucije." *Novosti.rs,* 11 May 2011,http://www.novosti.rs/vesti/planeta.70. html: 330060-Niksic-Pronadjena-dva-bezivotna-tela (accessed: 29 Dec. 2011).

11 The announcement can be accessed at Blagojević, Slađan, "Dom Revolucije - Ruglo Koje Niko Neće," *Online Vijesti,* 14 May 2011, http://www.vijesti.me/vijesti/dom-revolucije-ruglo-koje-niko-nece-clanak-19792 (accessed: 29 Dec. 2011).

former Yugoslavia. The idea of the *internal transfer* of knowledge between developed and not developed republics in Yugoslavia was clear. Beyond idealistic goals of socialism, such as centralism, this transfer of knowledge transpired chiefly as pragmatic. Cutting its ties to Stalinism and having limited access to Western democracies, Yugoslavia with its roughly twenty million inhabitants presented a sizable market that only needed to be turned around. In theory this *pragmatic* idea of decentralization was in line with *dialectical materialism* focusing on socialist production rather than idealism. The concept of dialectical materialism is well known as the Marxian interpretation of reality that views "matter as the sole subject of change and all change as the product of a constant conflict between opposites arising from the internal contradictions inherent in all events, ideas, and movements." Yugoslav socialism interpreted it as a tool for decentralization. Yet it was criticized that instead of bringing ethnic differences together, in practice, Yugoslav pragmatism made the distinctions even stronger. Large resistance was coming mainly from Belgrade, Zagreb and Ljubljana in effect protecting their own construction markets and pronouncing pragmatism of transfer as naive. Still, architecture like the *Homes of the Revolution* in Montenegro by Slovenian and Croatian architects took some hold of reality. With the socialist ideology vanishing, it is the raw architecture (finished or unfinished) that reappears in surprising ways.

If the *Home of the Revolution* in Nikšić did not find its final resolution and usage with the declining socialist political system, the *Kolašin Memorial,* built in the Montenegrin mountains by the Morača River to honor the First Session of the Antifascist Council of Montenegro succeeded. The monument is inhabitable and used by the municipality in daily administration. Successfully merging monumentality with quotidian use is an

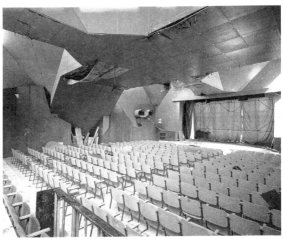

Kolašin Monument, Town Hall and Community Center,
Kolašin, Montenegro, Architects: Marko Mušić with
Gradimir Medaković, built 1974, photographed in 2010

intelligent approach to building for the future. There is, however, a lack of clarity about the single authorship for this workable memorial. Slovenian architect Marko Mušič and Gradimir Medaković – another prominent architect of the era – have both been credited with the design of the structure, as well as the prominent Yugoslav sculptor Dušan Džamonja. Regardless, the lasting impact of this memorial is the dual strategy of monumentation and administration.

Kolašin Memorial is a useful space of the everyday for the municipality. The mix of the symbolic and the everyday have proved pragmatic. According to historian Peter Krečič, Marko Mušič "accepted certain initiatives of regionalism" in his plan for a memorial center in Kolašin. The *Kolašin Memorial* was the point of transition towards an organic architecture that Mušič later used in designing religious commissions in Slovenia.[12] Mušič, an apprentice to the well-known postwar architect Louis Kahn, invested himself in the emotional aspects of building, and no doubt battled the collective forces of spirituality vis-à-vis socialism. According to the biography of Marko Mušič that was published by the Slovenian Academy of Arts and Sciences, the architect and academic had a large percentage of commissions for "sacral facilities and arrangements" and sacral "memorials" as compared to the number of civic commissions for the Yugoslav and Slovenian states.[13] As socialism vanished after the death of Tito, insecurity about the future affected

12 Krečič, Peter, "Architecture in Former Yugoslavia," Dubravka Djurić and Miško Šuvaković (eds.), *Impossible Histories: Historical Avant-gardes, Neo-avant-gardes, and Post-avant-gardes in Yugoslavia, 1918–1991,* Cambridge, MA: MIT, 2006, 360–1.

13 See: "Marko Marijan Mušič," *Aktualni Dogodki – Slovenska Akademija Znanosti in Umetnosti – Sazu.si,* Slovenska Akademija Znanosti I Umetnosti / SAZU, http://www.sazu.si/clani/marko-marijan-music (accessed: 30 Dec. 2011).

everyday life and began to shape collective behavior. Kolašin's *Memorial* mastery lies in the combination of the two forces – vanished symbolism and emerging pragmatism of the everyday – in the same work of architecture.

The achievement of capturing both the centripetal and centrifugal aspects of *Balkanization* in one building is rare. The architecture of the *Kolašin Memorial* is unique among the scores of abandoned monuments form late socialism in Yugoslavia. We can claim that the majority of structures suffered a fate of uselessness for failing to amalgamate multiple uses into a singular strategy. This is not to say that socialist monuments did not have a social program, which they did. However their social program was based on Kardelj's *timelessness* of decentralized socialism, rather than Todorova's concept of *timeliness* and everyday needs *Balkanising* away. When these two parallel concepts were sewn into an architecture in full observation of socialist ideology, they failed. When these concepts were set in amalgamated dissonance of programs, or *timeliness,* their concurrent nature kept architecture in use, such as in the *Memorial* in Kolašin.

The inhabited memorial in Kolašin is a rare example where the everyday and the memory of ideology alternate, thus keeping it in use. Most of the socialist memorials and institutions became vacant and abandoned. One of them is the little known *Kosturnica* (Bone repository) monument in the small town of Kavadarci, in Macedonia. The memorial guards and marks the location of the remains of the anti-fascist partisan fighters from World War II. Designed by the locally-born painter Petar Mazev, the monument is processional in sequence and sits atop a strategic hill where one can easily imagine the battle. Mazev is described as "A follower of American *neoexpressionism* and one of the most important postwar painters who introduced new energy into contemporary Macedonian art".[14] The monument complex is both sculpted and engineered in brutal concrete. The Macedonian version of *brutalism* became a local specialty after Kenzo Tange's reconstruction of Skopje in the late 1960s and early 1970s.

The transfer of knowledge (especially engineering and seismology) from Japan to Macedonia is evident in this memorial. Symbolically, *Kosturnica* evokes a frozen flower in a cantilevered single structure in concrete with a pre-classically influenced open air space for rituals situated alongside it. After the *vanishing act* of Yugoslav socialism and the independence of Macedonia in the early 1990s, the *Kosturnica* monument lost its public role. In the rapid deterioration of Yugoslav socialism, politics in Macedonia were occupied with carving territorial identity out of Yugoslavia rather than observing rituals based on socialist memory. Ideological rituals were quickly replaced by the urgency of the everyday. Today, like an artificial concrete rock on a hill, *Kosturnica* is accessible more than ever intended, without any processional nor ideological demands.

Petrova Gora in Croatia is one of many languishing memorials from the socialist era of the former Yugoslavia. Conceived in 1981 by Vojin Bakić, a Croatian sculptor who won many state-funded commissions, working with the architect Branislav Šerbetić, the project was designed as a 12-story-tall social center, set on the site of a partisan field hospital used during World War II. Finally completed in 1989 as a monument to Yugoslavia's resistance fighters, the memorial was used as intended for only a brief period before the eruption of the Balkan crisis. The wars that ensued scattered refugees around the region,

14 See: *DLUM,* Association of Artists of Macedonia, 2007, http://www.dlum.org.mk/en/osnovopoloznik.asp?id=13 (accessed: 8 Aug. 2012).

Srdjan Jovanovic Weiss with Armin Linke

Kosturnica Memorial, Prilep, Macedonia, Artists and
Architects: Petar Mazev and Petar Muličkovski, built 1976,
photographed in 2009

practically erasing the political cause this structure was meant to embody.

Today, *Petrova Gora* stands unused and empty, but open, thanks to the neglect passively offered by Croatia's democratic government. Anyone can come here, enter the site, walk inside the monument, and wander upward through twelve interconnected levels all the way to the roof. In fact, the near-by residents have already appropriated the material surface of the memorial by pealing off its titanium panels and taking them away.

The feeling of melancholy inspired by *Petrova Gora* is overwhelming, but it is irresistible to call it beautiful. Furthermore, an astonishing aspect of this monument is that its interior is the size of a small Guggenheim museum, positioned on a dramatic hilltop site. It is also significant that the building is the work of an abstract artist, and that the site's architect played only a minor role.

Contemporary artists have discovered this inhabitable monument and are embracing *Petrova Gora* in their work. Take the video produced by David Maljković, which portrays the structure far in the future as a neglected fiction. Other projects and expeditions to the site have produced similar imagery, evoking "nostalgia for the future."

All of these projects raise awareness about this exceptional work, and about the exceptionality of Yugoslav socialism when compared to the idolatry of the Soviet Bloc. However, these artists' projects fail to ignite strategic thinking and analysis, especially within the context of contemporary practice, about ideologies deploying art in place of design. Moreover, little if no work has been done to relate this monument to the American influence upon Yugoslav cultural policies during the Cold War, making Yugoslavia an ally to the West and offsetting the Soviet East. American abstract art, conceptual art, and corporate architecture

Srdjan Jovanovic Weiss with Armin Linke

Petrova Gora Memorial, Petrova Gora, Croatia,
Artists and Architects: Vojin Bakić and Branislav Šerbetić,
built 1989, photographed in 2011

all play provocative roles in this history. While some artists exhaust the repertoire of visual interventions, the time is ripe for architects to step in.

Yet time is also limited for further action. Visitors to *Petrova Gora* have already spotted men with geodesic equipment measuring the site of the memorial and the monument itself. This may mean that we are already late on the scene, and that there is perhaps little time to think of a strategy to put this monument back in the future, either for an authentic use (which few would fund without a neoliberal zeal for profit returns), or preserved as a beautiful ruin.

Other monuments built during the period of late Yugoslav socialism could have met a similar fate as the *Kavadarci, Kosturnica* and *Petrova Gora* memorials. The post-socialist governments in former Yugoslavia reprogrammed a few selected memorials, or re-idealized their prescribed content of commemorating the fallen partisan fighters of World War II. These efforts originate from state forces who suddenly found themselves in the position to answer to ethnic, if not nationalist tendencies of each new post-Yugoslavian state. Through these national governments, the *centrifugal* forces of the *architecture of Balkanization* have found a balance of interpretation of memory from socialist resistance to the Nazi occupation in WWII. By infusing national narratives into socialist memorials, a select number of them are kept in the lingering state between life and death. What follows are the two examples that went through the recoding programming of their initial purpose: *Ilinden Memorial* in Macedonia and *Bubanj Park* from Serbia.

According to the Yugoslav socialist codex, there were three dimensions to achieving abstract representation of ideology when dealing with the national sentiment: 1. Democratization of art; 2. Synthesis of plasticity in art; 3. Free form as the product of the contemporary visual aesthetic mind.[15] The memorial that is said to embody all three is the *Ilinden Memorial,* or also referred to as *Macedonium (Македониум).* It was built in 1974 in the Macedonian town of Kruševo at 1280 meters above the sea. This memorial had a double function. It was intended to commemorate the birth of the national uprising of the Macedonians against the Ottoman Empire in 1903 as well as to commemorate the local victims in the victory of Yugoslav partisans over the fascists in World War II.

As the *Ilinden Monument* was intended to symbolize both the antifascist liberation of the Macedonian homeland after World War II and to evoke the local uprising against the Turkish occupation in 1903, its agenda for memorialization was two-fold. Built in 1974, the monument is designed by the architect-artist couple Iskra and Jordan Grabul with the help of an engineer from Skopje. Ostensibly designed to emotionally move its visitors, *Ilinden* is an expressive mix of spatial sequencing, abstraction and social geometry. The memorial itself is designed as a landscape sequence departing from a local cemetery towards a top of a strategic hill where the battles, both against the Turks and against the Germans, allegedly took place. The sequence is composed in four distinct parts creating an eclectic promenade. The first part of the sequence, inspired by American minimalist art of the early 1970s, is an arrangement of oversized horseshoe-like shapes marking the passage. The second part of the sequence is arranged as a passage through an area of memorial plates. The third part of the sequence further up the hill is a clearance with an array of cylindrical tombstone-like pedestals forming an auditorium for

15   See: Jovanoski, Nikola, *Ilinden Monument,* Kruševo: DOOEL "Čiča" Center for Foreign Languages and Informatics, "InfoLIMB", 2000; in Macedonian: Јованоски, Никола, *Споменикот Илинден,* Крушево: ДООЕЛ "Чича", Центар са странски јазици и информатика, "ИнфоЛИМБ", 2000.

service or ceremonies. The fourth and final part of the memorial sequence is a large-scale cenotaph, the actual *Ilinden Monument*. The cenotaph's geometry is in the shape of an immense asterisk, a ball protruded by a spherical array of skylights that projects outside of the sphere in all directions. The centerpiece itself is an expressive conflation of engineering and art practice. A long central ramp takes the visitors directly into the center of the sphere, from which the interior is experienced as a church-like environment. Four horizontal skylights are reserved for the relief work that in some abstract way "depict" the four stages of the uprising of the Macedonian nation from "birth" to "maturity". The futuristic geometry of the monument is grounded by the church with vitrages commissioned from the artist Borko Lazeski. These add to the overall sense of the yet-unfound spirituality of socialism, somewhat of an anathema to the former Yugoslav regime. The Grabuls themselves were engaged in spiritualism rather than religion, finding the emotional space to be the driver of addressing the emotions of the uprising nation.

Constructed in 1974, the year in which Yugoslavia's new constitution gave Tito and Kardelj more power in exchange for sovereignty of the federal units, the *Ilinded Monument* is one of the first *national* monuments constructed in socialism. The duality between *socialist* and *national* segments of the memorial is rendered invisible. However each is given a performative role. Socialist policy of abstraction and technological advance was given to engineering, while the abstract expression of the national sentiment was given to artists (Josip Grabul and Borko Lazeski). The architect thus had only a nodal point of managing the scientific (engineering) and the artistic expressions in a dual mix.

The *vanishing act of socialism* here offers insights into the highest form of interchangeability between *socialism* and *nationalism*. The definitions of these have both been in a state of fluctuation

Srdjan Jovanovic Weiss with Armin Linke

Ilinden Monument, Kruševo, Macedonia,
Artists and Architects: Iskra and Jordan Grabul,
built 1974, photographed in 2009

since the end of the First World War and the retreat by the Ottoman Empire from the continent, especially in a young Macedonia, oscillating between the newly-found sense of ethnicity within Yugoslavia's socialist state and socialism within the ethnic republic. Observing the strategy with which the *Ilinden Monument* was created – by giving neither a focal point – we notice the duality of expressions that appears negotiable and interchangeable in Kardelj's dream. However, after the dissolution of Yugoslavia and the declaration of Macedonia as an independent democracy, the vanishing of socialism gave access to an occupation of one within the other. Today's authorities decipher the intentions of this monument to the public through a didactic approach including data and images that explain the monument's creation and supposed meaning. They do it by arranging a set of movable pin-up boards that flank the perimeter of the interior of the *Ilinden Monument.* Even though one can complain about the ruination of socialist abstraction, these didactic additions cannot measure up to the scale of the socialist monument. The immensity of engineering and abstraction that shape the *Ilinden Monument* are overpowering adjustments of its content. Thus the *vanishing act of socialism* reappears in the overpowering effects of extraordinary engineering and can absorb contemporary renditions of re-emerging national sentiment.

The *reappearing act of socialism,* when experienced at the larger scale of a memorial rather than a single structure, becomes less susceptible to the adjusted readings of its meanings. Unlike the *Ilinden Monument,* where the two narratives (one *socialist* and another *national*) are concurrent, *Bubanj Memorial Park* was built solely to commemorate the execution of more than 10,000 citizens of Niš and people from Serbia by the German forces during World War II. Thus *Bubanj* has a singular narrative over a much larger expanse. The park was completed in 1963 on a territory of 59 hectares. The centerpiece of *Bubanj* is in the shape of three oversized fists. The three fists, designed by the Croatian sculptor Ivan Sabolić, are grossly enlarged and cast in concrete. The surface is *tattooed* with scars in cement. The fists form the backdrop of an open air theatre and symbolize an untamable resistance. Every October 14th until the fall of socialism, scores of pupils from Serbia were bussed to *Bubanj* for a field trip to mark the *Liberation Day* of Niš. Once there, they were told that the tallest fist in concrete represents men, the middle fist represents women and the shortest fist represents the youth executed there during the Nazi occupation. The plateau in front of the monument has space for 10,000, symbolizing the number of people who were executed and buried.

Since the end of socialism, *Bubanj Memorial Park* emerged in public view as a place to by-pass the ideology simply by using it as a park. An immense and generous territory, it became frequented by everyday visitors, young families and their children. The very large scale of the memorial park has proven to be too big of a territory to be converted into anything else. Its size works in favor of its preservation. At the same time, Serbian and local government finds itself preoccupied with the repair of damage caused by Milošević-era economic policies which allowed criminals to become a dominant market sector. As a result of attention and energy spent elsewhere, *Bubanj Memorial Park* lives in a state of neglect. In fact, it is the state of neglect that keeps the memorial park open to all. The vanishing of socialism reappears in the common and spontaneous non-ideological use of the open space by the country's citizens.

Today the *Bubanj Memorial Park* is a favorite field-trip destination for Niš residents, especially on May 1st, *International Day of Labour*. The vastness of the memorial park territory preserves this land from being commercially exploited. Speculatively, the size of the park de-sacralizes the nostalgic memory of socialism

Bubanj Memorial Park, commemorating the anti-fascist
resistance in World War II, Niš, Serbia,
Artist: Ivan Sabolić, built 1963, photographed in 2010

of its ritualistic, almost *sacral* ideological elements. Said differently, the process of stripping away the spiritual aspects from this socialist memorial happens through a voluntary and civil profanation of use. Yet at the same time, the ongoing de-sacralization of the memorial is not showing through as the de-socialization of the park. The territory turns from memorial to recreational, where paths walked and crossed are different from the ones intended. During the killing fields between 1942–44, walking patterns were controlled in yet not fully known patterns by the German perpetrators, executioners and gravediggers for mass burial. During the period between the end of World War II and 1963, a burial pyramid was erected to commemorate the dead. Very little is known about the walking patterns of commemoration. After 1963, new walking patterns occupied the park with a larger and more sequenced territory of the memorial where bus tours would pour in pupils from all over Yugoslavia to "experience" a didactic walking pattern and culminate in the open air auditorium with the three fists of resistance as the backdrop. Today, walking patterns are non-prescribed and open for civilian use without the need to follow any didactic sequence. Thus the profanation of this partisan memorial park is not only a form of *de-sacralization* of a land containing thousands of buried bodies in mass graves, it is a form a self-organized transfusion of the territory of the memorial into a place that is a necessity for everyday and *timely* needs.

The *timeliness* as an aspect of *Balkanization* was clearly addressed in Kardelj's rotational key for architectural and urban commissions. We can extract a theory that Todorova's *timeliness* of *centrifugal Balkanization* meets Kardelj's strategic attempt in the rotational *timing* of commissions. He was hoping for the *centripetal* effect to meet the *centrifugal* architecture of *Balkanization*. Memorial parks like *Bubanj* – built in Serbia by a Croatian artist – are architectural places that were meant as a block between the forces of *Balkanization* and suggest the possibility of a lasting balance. We have seen how the *Memorial Home* in Kolašin survived the vanishing act of socialism simply because the memorial is inhabited not only by memory, but by the everyday needs for an administration. In the parks like *Bubanj,* this program, other than memorialization, is secured by their use as a place of everyday recreation.

The Yugoslav *rotational key* also allowed Belgrade architects access to major commissions for memorials to partisan victory and losses in World War II in other republics, such as Croatia, and Bosnia and Herzegovina. Architect Bogdan Bogdanović, to whom an entire separate study should be devoted, was both a privileged communist in political power structures and a dissident in his practice. World War II and the communist victory over fascism cemented distinct ethnic fragments into a singular, Yugoslav memory of resistance. As Lidija Merenik, critic and contemporary art historian from Belgrade, wrote, socialist "Yugoslavia early got rid of socialist realism as the official art" leaving abstraction to reign over figuration. The Yugoslav socialist use of abstraction in art and architecture was there to act as a force against the *Balkanization* of the country into ethnic parts. This approach to solidifying memory in abstraction remained in vogue long after World War II. Yet, as Merenik remarks, both social realism and figuration have been "hidden below a carpet" and left unattended, until it made a gradual and then explosive comeback during late socialism, violent crisis and its aftermath.[16] Bogdanović was a rare architect and artist who dared to use figurative (masterfully abstracted) motif in his architectural work for the partisan memorials. His largest and most prominent work expands the idea of partisan or ethnic victims to the memory of

16 Merenik, Lidija, "The Yugoslav Experience, Or What Happened To Socialist Realism," *Moscow Art Magazine* 28 (1998): n. pag.

the holocaust. This work is Bogdanović's design of the former concentration camp *Jasenovac* in eastern Croatia, then reworked into a large memorial park. The *Jasenovac Memorial Park* thus consists of an expansive landscape design of the grounds of the concentration camp and a monument in the form of an abstracted flower. The actual locations of the mass graves were marked by round land formations made of soft reams and earthen craters. The heart of the memorialization lies in the architectural sculpture, *The Flower*, which also houses a memorial center. *The Flower* was completed in 1968 as a large-scale, symbolic commemoration of the victims of the crime in Jasenovac. It also invited discussion of the politics of social symbolism and inspired the search for icons other than abstraction. Tito was reported to have attacked abstract art as a "dark wave" in film.[17] Indeed, Bogdan Bogdanović was a known dissident. However, under *soft* socialism, authorities who preferred figuration nevertheless sponsored abstraction, and Bogdanović used this key moment to unmask hidden socialist *desire* for classical architecture and figurative art. This *desire,* implemented by Stalin as the Soviet neo-classical architecture already before socialist Yugoslavia existed, was largely a taboo in Tito's postwar Yugoslavia. Thus the concepts embedded in *The Flower* seem to run on two distinct levels: one towards improving on abstraction as a form of social amalgamation and the other one to unmask the Yugoslav socialist policy that saw non-communist symbolism as taboo. The material metaphor in the architecture and the engineering of *The Flower* in concrete prevailed.[18]

17 Ibid.

18 This is not the only example where a communist architect, usually dealing with architectural or abstract geometries proposed literal, figurative and non-abstract monuments for leftist systems. From Le Corbusier's hand in Chandigarh to Oscar Niemeyer's monuments in Brasília.

Jasenovac Memorial to the victims of World War II
concentration camp, Jasenovac, Croatia,
Architect: Bogdan Bogdanović, built 1966,
photographed in 2011

The *vanishing act* of socialism in the 1980s and 1990s left the *Jasenovac Memorial* abandoned and unmaintained. In 2009, *The Flower* was partly repaired and re-inagurated, not as a memorial to the Jewish holocaust, but to all "victims in the antifascist struggle". The question is: Is *The Flower* a materialized *idea* of *socialist architecture,* or mere *architecture from socialism?* The *reappearing idea* of *socialism* will move us closer to Kardelj's *strategic* and Todorova's *analytic* relationship to the *centripetal* and the *centrifugal* forces of *Balkanization,* balanced within the dissidence of Bogdanović's architectural and sculptural spatial practice. Here we need to remark that ideological architecture has been debated in the case of neo-classical architecture in both nationalist and socialist systems in history such as Hitler's or Stalin's. It is generally accepted that through the release of Albert Speer, architect for the Third Reich, there is no *National Socialist* architecture, only architecture in the *National Socialist* period. On the other hand, the case of architecture in the Soviet Union is presented in the thesis by Alexei Tarkhanov and Sergei Kavtaradze as *Stalinist architecture* and as the *materialized idea* of *socialist architecture.*[19] Thus, in order to be critical for the discourse of the *architecture of Balkanization, socialist architecture* alone is investigated as an *idea of socialist architecture* solidified in architectural or landscape material.[20] The question remains: does the vanishing *idea* of socialist ideology leave us with *socialist architecture* alone?

19 See: Tarkhanov, Alexei, and Sergei Kavtaradze, *Stalinist Architecture,* London: Laurence King, 1992.

20 Piškor/Epeha, Mate, "Predsjednik Mesić U Jasenovcu: U Hrvatskoj i Europi Nema Mjesta Za Ljude Koji Veličaju Fašizam," *Slobodna Dalmacija,* 26 Apr. 2009, http://www.slobodnadalmacija.hr/Hrvatska/tabid/66/articleType/ArticleView/articleId/52010/Default.aspx (accessed: 9 Aug. 2012).

In order to come closer to the idea of *socialist architecture*, I propose to use the concept of *timeliness* of *Balkanization* as it was
previously attended via Todorova. The *timeliness,* versus *timelessness*, separates spatial and political moments in the timing of *Balkanization*. This is analogous to the geo-political understanding
of *Balkanization* as the process of hostile separation in space and
territory alone. *Timeliness* helps us differentiate what I propose
calling *territorial time zones*. My expectation is that by establish-
ing *time zones* of *Balkanization, socialist architecture* emerges when
the *idea* of *socialist architecture* vanishes. This could be called
socialist archaeology, however archaeology may be a misleading
term for an idea of socialism, versus antiquity and dead civi-
lizations. Here we assume that *socialism* is not dead, but that it
has been mutating from a fixed to a more *elastic*, flexible arena.
When it is rooted in the future, like the vanguard, its *elasticity*
lets the idea of socialism appear, often in unexpected forms.
Or to have the very same forms and materials, like the memorials, become read in a *timely* manner, and perhaps as naked
landscape. This idea of *nakedness* and *elasticity* of post-socialism
is thoroughly researched in Katherine Verdery's anthropological account of neighboring Romania.[21] I think that it can be
partly used to address the vanishing act of socialism in the former Yugoslavia, and its reappearance in its multiple futures,
in various, or staggered moments in time. Verdery's question,
and the eponymous book *What Was Socialism And What Comes
Next?*, looks at socialism as a serpent that is changing its skin,
however has not enough time for it, and appears *naked.*[22] This
anthropological model of reading, when applied on the timely

---

21 Verdery, Katherine, "The Elasticity of Land: Problems of
    Property Restitution in Transylvania," *What Was Socialism,
    and What Comes Next?*, Princeton, NJ: Princeton UP, 1996,
    134–67.

22 Ibid., 229–34.

reading of abandoned memorials and monuments as objects without the new skin, can allow for a material reading of architecture, rather than an *ideological* one.

Bogdan Bogdanović's earlier work in the city of Mostar in Bosnia and Herzegovina gives some information about the *naked* issue of *time* coming out of late socialism when architecture was allowed its often introverted play. Bogdanović's *Partisan Memorial Cemetery* in Mostar was a commission that came before the commission for his memorial of the World War II concentration camp in Jasenovac. The preparatory site work for *Partisan Memorial Cemetery* began in 1960. Land located on the north slope of the so called "Bishop's Hill" was formally obtained through nationalization in March 1961. The *Partisan Memorial Cemetery* opened in 1965 and was attended by Josip Broz Tito. Tito pronounced it *beautiful*. More than a commemorative space, the *Partisan Memorial Cemetery* also served as the site for young pioneer induction ceremonies where Yugoslav children recited their pledges to the country and its socialist course.

What makes Bogdanović's design for the *Partisan Memorial Cemetery* in Mostar distinct is the unprecedented use of the expansive spatial sequence to re-materialize the idea of memory in a socialist system. The sequence starts with an all but ambiguous trench formation in stone with two concurrent walking passages on both its sides. The sequence morphs into a wide hill-like promenade for walking around simulations of fortress structures and densely planted horticulture. Then the visitor enters into a recreation of what appears like an archetypal village with walls on both sides evoking a medieval town. The visitor arrives at the top of the complex where the view of Mostar opens up. The layering of the walls made to look like supporting the ground from not sliding off the hill creates a central point of the memorial. The stepping stone looking elements dispersed on the ground

Partisan Memorial Cemetery, Mostar, Bosnia and
Herzegovina, Architect: Bogdan Bogdanović, built 1965,
photographed in 2010

represent the imaginary locations of the individual graves of the partisans.[23]

Here finally, we can detect an attempt of Yugoslav *soft socialism* to use architecture to match the *centrifugal* forces of *Balkanization*. In this memorial this was done via the sequential, almost theatrical, architecture of the arrival to the *Partisan Memorial Cemetery* up on the hill in Mostar. Thus Bogdanović uses the time that it takes to experience the architectural sequence, which is significant, in order to have a centripetal effect of gathering for anyone or any group using it. In terms of the effort to introduce architecture as the *centripetal* force of collective experience, this effort of building the *Partisan Memorial Cemetery* is the most extensive one. The analysis of the *Partisan Memorial Cemetery* tells us that architecture was used in order to create a larger *centripetal* force as opposed to the *centrifugal* force of *Balkanization*. The visitor sequence of Bogdanović's memorial in Mostar is *centrifugal*. As it meanders, this walking sequence is fragmentary and perpetually particular in its meaning. On the other hand, the use of stone craft for wall surfaces and iconic doorways is *centripetal*. This craft unites the fragments into a "city". Thus, Mostar memorial amalgamates the double nature of *architecture of Balkanization* into one space.

Late socialism in Yugoslavia did not only provide the idea of the practice that architecture can be deployed as the counterbalance to ethnic separation and overall *Balkanization*. It also showed us that the scale of such operation can go up from the industrial design, architectural, landscape, urban to the scale of designing new cities. And it is the opportunity to scale up design efforts to the size of the city that can color *Balkanization* in a more strategic way than that it has been looked at

23 Linke, Armin, and Srdjan Jovanovic Weiss, "Partisan Memorial Cemetery," Tobia Bezzola (ed.), *Socialist Architecture: The Vanishing Act,* Zurich: JRP/Ringier, 2011, 116–18.

before. To remind us, Todorova warned that *Balkanization* has not yet gained its remedial side, and that it is *tarrying with the negative.*[24] *Balkanization* presented only as the *imaginary,* or the *metaphorical,* discourse seems to mask the particular achievements of its own *architecture* on the ground.

Through a set of unexpected circumstances, the city in Yugoslavia that drew sudden international focus was Skopje, the capital of Macedonia. In 1963, Skopje suffered a major earthquake that demolished large parts of the city. The city was then re-planned and gradually renovated by Japanese brutalist architect Kenzo Tange in (often turbulent) collaboration with the planners from the Croatian Planning Institute from Zagreb. In a contemporary context, the Republic of Macedonia today is one of the successor states of the former Yugoslavia from which it declared independence in 1992. It became a member of the United Nations in 1993.

The Skopje earthquake happened after Bogdanović received the commission for the *Partisan Memorial Cemetery* in Mostar and before the cemetery was inaugurated. Even though there is no direct correlation between these two events, Yugoslavia at large was suddenly faced with the situation of having to rebuild and commemorate at the same time. The mid-1960s was a high watermark for urban planning, new city construction and the development of infrastructure such as the *Highway of Brotherhood and Unity,* all of which took significant attention away from the architecture of commemoration. This literally left open the field for experimentation with abstracted aesthetics. Bogdanović's soft, nostalgic aesthetics, appealed as *romantic, emotion-driven* and *understandable* to a common citizen. His use of natural and classical symbols reflects a sharp turn from rational and modern aesthetics, away from communist symbols such as the red star. The earthquake in Skopje perhaps triggered this sharp turn

---

24 See: Žižek, Slavoj, *Tarrying with the Negative: Kant, Hegel, and the Critique of Ideology,* Durham: Duke UP, 1993.

by having the presence of Kenzo Tange and the new brutalist aesthetics directly implemented as a state, if not an ideological project in itself. Consistent with Yugoslav maneuvering between capitalism and Stalinism during the cold war, the "third way" may have been more appealing than stark modernism nor equally stark Stalinist neoclassical architecture.

Skopje needed to be rebuilt quickly after the earthquake, efficiently and convincingly prepared for any further seismographic disturbances. Meanwhile, Yugoslavia was handing out multiple commissions for partisan memorials, museums and homes of the revolution. Commissioning the rebuilding of an entire city certainly had to relate the importance of inhabitation as related to symbolism. This we can also interpret as two concurrent projects of *urgency* parallel to a kind of architectural art in search for *soft socialist aesthetics,* brutal urban engineering versus the aesthetic surface of memory.

The natural disaster that destroyed large parts of Skopje in 1963 was used to rethink the existing socialist planning in Yugoslavia. The plan was backed by Tito, the Yugoslav Communist Party, and the United Nations. The ongoing projects for New Belgrade and New Zagreb were showing signs of *Balkanization* due to conflict between Serbian and Croatian architects and urbanists. Thus, one can propose a sub-thesis to the *architecture of Balkanization,* that commissioning Kenzo Tange and his Japanese team was primarily a political decision. This political decision was fostering centripetal forces of *Balkanization,* using a distant international practice to neutralize any centrifugal forces of *Balkanization.*

In Skopje, we can test the basic thesis of Todorova's conclusion about the *incompleteness* of *Balkanization.* Her conclusion reads that the imaginary of *Balkanization* has an exclusive and negative meaning of conflict and war, and that it does not have its positive counterpoint. To repeat: "If Europe has produced not only

Above: Kenzo Tange, model of the Master Plan for the
Reconstruction of Skopje City Center,
Skopje, Macedonia, 2009

Below: Kenzo Tange, Urban Planning Institute,
Skopje, Macedonia, 2009

racism but also antiracism, not only misogyny but also feminism, not only anti-Semitism, but also repudiation, then what can be termed Balkanism has not been coupled with its complement-ing and ennobling antiparticle."[25] Not yet. However, emerging usages of the term point to *positive aspects of Balkanization.* They are referring to the power of self-determination, self-organiza-tion, urban self-regulation, aspects of territorial distinction and finally creating new capital cities, such as Skopje. The emergence of this new capital city in South East Europe vis-à-vis its late socialist destiny and rebuilding takes architecture and urban planning into the center of the discourse. It may hold some clues to both experience in rebuilding a city in a post-disaster stage as well as knowledge about Kenzo Tange's approach, his promises and eventual set-backs of the renovation process in general.[26]

"It is a chilled evening after a very hot day that have just passed over Skopje. We are visiting Skopje's Main Railway Station de-signed by Kenzo Tange four decades after it was built. The bulky locomotive, painted in red with white and yellow stripes, pulls a passenger train out of the station. The composition is small, only three passenger cars are tagged behind the locomotive. The de-parture is on time. The destination is north. The train leaves for the seven hour voyage to Belgrade and rumbles over the elevated tracks. Several bright spotlights glare over the platform of the

25 Todorova, Maria, *Imagining the Balkans,* New York: Oxford UP, 1997. 187.

26 Even though I grew up and was educated in Yugoslavia, Skopje was never my city of residence. However precisely a year before the devastating earthquake occurred in 1963, my father started studying architecture in Skopje. Like many he had to leave the city after the earthquake and since then he retained emotional ties to the city. Four and a half decades later I took a few trips to Skopje on various artistic projects and initiatives like the *Lost Highway Expedition* in 2006 and *Forum Skopje* in 2009, and this last time I brought Armin Linke to photograph the traces of the renovation.

station. Not all the lights are working. The Swiss railway clocks hang each on a series of concrete towers that are marking the exit away from the station. Each clock is showing a different time. Looking at this, we may be thinking that we are in the city that operates in multiple time zones simultaneously."[27] The un-synchronized times on the clocks at Skopje Railway Station can then be read as a symbol of *distinct timeliness, Balkanized time zones* that operated both in the former socialist Yugoslavia, and today.

As mentioned earlier, this railway station was built according to the plans of 1966 by Kenzo Tange and his Japanese team of what became known worldwide as the *brutalist architects.* In spite of the fact that only one tenth of the original design was constructed, the station shows principles of Tange's spatial strategy: mark the perimeter by a wall or an interpretation of the wall and let it *breathe* through a system of openings and gates.

A close view of the original model for the master plan of Skopje by Kenzo Tange reveals the proposed strategy for the reconstruction of the city in the 1960s. Strategically and financially, the United Nations led efforts to reconstruct Skopje in close collaboration with the then-socialist Yugoslav government and its lifetime president Josip Broz Tito. Tito welcomed the UN's funds and pronounced Skopje the "City of Solidarity". Donations included not only physical construction materials, but also shared ideas and planning. Reported as early as 1964 by the Journal of American Planning Association, the idea of solidarity was reflected through a rumor that the Yugoslavs would ideally like to see the city rebuilt through the good will of foreign countries. "Thus four blocks of Washington Street might then turn into Lenin Street along the area of Soviet donation, followed by DeGaulle Avenue." Some ideas of centrifugal *Balkanization* were also floated "that the oriental character of the city be eliminated, that the

27 Jovanovic Weiss, Srdjan, and Armin Linke, "Skopje Will Disappear," *Abitare*, July 2010: 83–95.

gypsies, Albanians, and Turks, be transferred to other parts of the Macedonian Republic."[28]

To prevent any such scenarios from taking place during the rebuilding of Skopje, the United Nations and socialist Yugoslavia negotiated the creation of an international design competition. The winning prize awarded to Tange was partly shared with the *Croatian Town Planning Institute*. Tange drew praise for his vision of the modern city based on an inner core, arrangement of infrastructure, provision of openness, and the reconstruction of the city's memory through the placement of key buildings in a procession called "The City Wall". The Croatian team was hailed for its knowledge of the conditions on the ground as well as economy and experience of Yugoslav reconstruction. An unlikely combination of collaborators, the office of Kenzo Tange and the Croatian team of experts after many conflicts and iterations eventually produced the "Ninth Project" with additional input from the other competitions entries. The group reached a consensus on the plan for the city's future in 1966. The original model was then built in Tange's office in Japan in four segments before being sent to Skopje for exhibition.

In all its expanse and solidarity-themed symbolism, the reconstruction of Skopje can be read as the monument, memorial in its own *timeliness* of construction. However, it is not considered an aesthetic experience, or memorial, like the *Partisan Memorial Cemetery* or other memorials by Bogdan Bogdanović. The scale of operations in Skopje privileged a sense of urgency in the engineering and calculated rationalization of the reconstruction. So much so, that the focus on memory was shifted to efficiency and basic functions of the city.

Except for one *instant* memorial. At the time of the implementation of Kenzo Tange's master plan, the conference room of

---

28 Fisher, Jack C. (1964), "The Reconstruction of Skopje," *Journal of the American Planning Association,* 30:1, 46–48.

Skopje's *Urban Planning Office* was in frequent use for visits by Josip Broz Tito, dignitaries, guests, and personnel from the United Nations. The actual room has remained intact since then and now serves as an impromptu memorial to the planning process for the reconstruction of Skopje. The walls of the room still hold the original prints of the land use management proposal by Tange. The scale model of one of the main segments of Tange's master plan are kept on the table in the middle of the room. The only *disruption* to the authentic elements of the memorial is the cheerful inscription on the wall, which reads: "Happy New Year 2009" in Macedonian.

This is where the previous ideas of *distinction,* within *late socialist* Yugoslavia, can find their spatial resolution. Kenzo Tange, as the distinctly Japanese architect and urban planner at the time contributed to the centripetal drive vis-à-vis ethnic *Balkanization* in Yugoslavia. The campaign of *solidarity* was introduced in order to re-make Skopje as an example of what Yugoslav *softened socialism* could achieve internationally. Thanks to this forgetfulness and neglect of the brutalist plan, Skopje can still offer the authentic, unfinished spaces of Kenzo Tange's master plan. The Skopje Main Railway station is one of those spaces. With the authorities looking away for decades nothing significant has been done to change, improve these infrastructures, or memorialize them. The instant memorial of the reconstruction of Skopje at the *Urban Planning Institute* is thus more original, more contemporary, and more accessible than any planned memorial would perhaps most likely be.

Kenzo Tange's master plan allowed the release of competitions for cultural buildings in the city center only to multi-ethnic Yugoslav architects. One of these competitions was won by the young Slovenian office Biro 71. Biro 71 was influenced by Finnish organic architecture, finding formal inspiration in nature. The building of the *Macedonian Opera and Ballet* was a radical proposal to begin with. But Biro 71 took this organic approach to a whole new level by designing a massive complex of cultural buildings next to Skopje's own river. The Yugoslav government built only a third of it. Today, it still stands as the *Macedonian Opera and Ballet* building. The Slovenian architects who designed the *Macedonian Opera and Ballet* building proved smart: they kept the nascent form of natural rock foundations, which they then solidified in concrete. Their opera was made in concrete. The building was painted white under post-socialist administration so it would look stone cladded. The building is similar to the Finlandia building of Alvar Aalto in Helsinki, performing a dual role as both a cultural and territorial icon. As a result, the building's shape is preserved and aging better than others in the city overall. The project did include set-backs. The original design for 1000 seats was scaled down to 300. Additionally, the authorities could build only one of the three proposed structures. The main auditorium has suffered from the severe reduction of seats due to budget cuts. Having little time to detail the seats, they were built on an incline following the complex geometry of the floor. Sitting inside feels like riding a downward-facing train. The radical functionality of scale embodied in the original proposal vanished. What has emerged in its place is the bodily phenomenon of a fast-moving Macedonian democracy.

Built in multiple stages between 1974 and 1989, the *Post Office* is the work of a Macedonian architect who returned to Skopje after the earthquake in 1963. Janko Konstantinov worked with Alvar Aalto prior to his homecoming and was a contemporary of another Macedonian architect who studied at Yale University with Paul Rudolf. Both architects brought to Skopje the use of raw concrete applied to institutional buildings. Yet nowhere is this use of raw material more imbued with romantic sentiment, curvilinearity, and a sense of compactness of form tailored for

Macedonian Opera and Ballet, Skopje, Macedonia,
Architect: Biro 71, built 1981, photographed in 2009

Srdjan Jovanovic Weiss with Armin Linke

Post Office, Skopje, Macedonia,
Architect: Janko Konstantinov, built 1974,
photographed in 2009

its interior use than in the *Post Office*. The bold use of reinforced concrete and expressive rounded forms makes the building a raw icon, both visually and in the proverbial public eye, especially in early stages of democracy. Konstantinov was supposedly inspired by the nearby medieval fortress, but popular rumors claim an altogether different natural source: an exotic flower grossly enlarged and frozen in concrete. Disagreement about the building's origin story aside, no one is left untouched by its appearance.

The rawness of the exterior stands in contrast to the more sensitive interior. The public postal areas, the main hall, and the telephone area were drawn to fit – if not capture – the public's use of the institutions in plain circular geometry evoking a church-like experience. Frescos by Borko Lazeski flank the sides of the rotunda space of the hall with postal tellers. The flower arrangements are likewise circular and carefully maintained. While this space is still in use, the adjacent rotunda housing the telephone area is now obsolete and out of use. Connected with repetitive round windows, the two rotundas seem to co-exist in asymmetrical opposition like two time capsules, one in the past, and one still in the present.

The brutalist movement took ground in Macedonia. This is most evident with this massive post office built by the Macedonian architect Janko Konstantinov between 1972–89. Built in three stages, this building complex takes the inspiration of nature and roughness brought by the Japanese architects to the level of national identity. The second best example is the Skopje Hydro-meteorological Station built by Kristo Todorovski in 1975. There are other brutalist building complexes, mostly institutions like the University of Skopje. They were heavily influenced by Paul Rudolf, the American brutalist architect, for whom they also worked. Together they contributed to Skopje becoming a *museum* of brutalist architecture, sculptural, rough-edged architecture, produced within the context of Yugoslavia's socialist political system. At the same time, Tange's infusion into Yugoslav late socialist mathematics upgraded the visibility of the Macedonian architectural scene, indistinguishable before the devastating earthquake.[29] The *brutalist museum* city of Skopje is already in danger of disappearing. In 2010, the government adopted an iconic plan called "Skopje 2014" to refashion the capital as "timeless" appearing to rise as from an imaginary antiquity.[30] This will largely destroy the openness and solidarity of Skopje that it was built on. Skopje's mixed population (ethnic Macedonians as the dominant demographic, but also large Albanian and Roma minorities) are using the same brutalist infrastructure. If the plans by the government go ahead as planned, Skopje will no longer be the city of the future as planned by Kenzo Tange and his Japanese team. Today, in the era of vanished ideology, the government in place wants to bury Tange's socialist backed plan and rebuild the Macedonian capital as a historical city tied to antiquity and the fictional times of Alexander the Great.

There is opposition to this simulation of history. It is strong, intellectual in nature and fragmented. This opposition, however creative, is in need of coordination and support. Activist groups like The *First Architecture Brigade, Forum Skopje* and artists taking inspiration from Skopje's brutalist past like Yane Čalovski, Hristina Ivanoska, Oliver Musovik, Filip Jovanovski and others are all united in the intellectual opposition to the current plan of

29 In comparison to Serbian, Croatian and Slovenian architects, Macedonian architects had very little exposure in socialist Yugoslavia before the earthquake in Skopje in 1963. Most talented ones departed for the US where they worked with modernist, and brutalist architects such as Paul Rudolf.

30 See: Perseytube, "Macedonia Timeless Capital Skopje2014," *YouTube,* 04 Feb. 2010, http://www.youtube.com/watch?v=iy-bmt-iLysU (accessed: 11 Aug. 2012).

the government. Architects Goran Janev and Blaž Križnik write smart contributions to public media about "closing on" the future of Skopje from being an open city to the "Grand National Capital". Jasmina Siljanovska, Professor at Skopje University and influential urbanist in Skopje, leads workshops to help grasp the magnitude of the transition towards the emerging democracy. They all share an analytical point of view, but are in need of a broader campaign that is capable of standing up to the powers in place. If the international community of architects and urbanists, and fans of Japanese urban history do not engage, we will be witnessing the radical erasure of brutalist urbanism, losing the experience of post-disaster reconstruction, destroying values of solidarity and mutual support in the process of rebuilding. Skopje will *disappear* again.

The discussion over the future of Skopje is ongoing and vibrant. Organizations like the *First Architectural Brigade* and *Forum Skopje* hold debates, create alternative city maps, and appear in the media seeking options for the future of their city other than those offered by the current establishment. However, even in these open debates far too often the role of Tange's reconstruction plan is invoked critically. The overall criticism is that this plan did not materialize enough in its scope 1. to be remembered and 2. to become the basis for future ideas to build upon. Additionally, the Japanese plan is seen historically as a top-down spatial experiment that re-organized the city into an unrecognizable territory for inhabitation; i.e. that it did not consider the forces and the mix of cultures on the ground as much as it could.

It is largely the case that Macedonian architects got inspired to respond, build and contribute to their own city more than anyone else in the new Macedonia. Today, the thesis that "the city should be left only to its own architects" is vacuous and represents the fake choice over other unexplored options of solidarity, internationality and exchange. Just as it was important to forge solidarity in the 1960s, it may be wise to initiate the powers of solidarity again. A promising option is to repurpose the original strategy of solidarity and open up the process to the international community of spatial practitioners. Theoretically this situation may initiate a new pragmatic call to the new generation of younger Japanese architects in Skopje's urban development. Emerging architectural offices like the Atelier Bow Wow, Tezuka Architects or Junya Ishigamy + Associates live with brutalist Japanese infrastructure and make it work. Indeed, as foreigners, they are well-positioned to by-pass the impasse of reconstruction left by Kenzo Tange and can serve as an example of the future role of an architect vis-à-vis an emerging democracy like Macedonia's.[31] The dissolution of Yugoslavia, the vanishing act of socialism, and the declaration of Macedonian independence in 1991 not only turned Skopje into the new capital of an independent country, it also brought about a shift from a centralized economy to a free market logic. Skopje's architecture adjusted to the new commercial interests and is in process of using popular and political power to forever bury the raw aesthetics of Kenzo Tange's vision. Yet, thanks to this forgetfulness and neglect of the Japanese plan, Skopje can still offer the authentic spaces of Kenzo Tange's master plan.

Besides the material masking of the experimental architecture of late socialism in Skopje, there is a latent historical masking of cultural *Balkanization* detectable in socialism by a single narrative. The notion of the *syncretic* attribute has been used recently to create a historical category of former Yugoslav modernist architecture. Architecture historians Maroje Mrduljaš and Vladimir Kulić presented the idea of *syncretic architecture* as part of the larger framework of Yugoslav geo-political "in-betweenness" during

---

31 Jovanovic Weiss, Srdjan, and Armin Linke, "Skopje Will Disappear," *Abitare*, July 2010: 83–95.

OXFAM

VAT: 348 4542 38

Volunteer here. Have fun,
meet new people & learn
new skills
Sign up in-store or at
www.oxfam.org.uk/joinheteam

| ERANTHIA | SALES | F8083/POS2 |

WEDNESDAY 7 DECEMBER 2022   18:01 004555
GIFT AID 20430086758083

| 1 | C9 - ARTS | £8.00 |

1 Items

| TOTAL | **£8.00** |
| CREDIT CARD | £8.00 |

F8083
48 Upper Street
Islington - N1 0PN
02073596020
oxfam.org.uk/shop

Share your finds with
#FoundInOxfam

THANK YOU

the Cold War.[32] The core of this investigation appears correct in terms of presenting a political unity from socialist Yugoslavia, having various, eclectic modern outputs, that as the authors say "remain unfinished". This is a compelling argument historically, in relation to the known thesis about unfinished modernism by Kenneth Frampton, and the unfinished ideological project of socialism by David Harvey. However, this thesis stays within the imaginary aspects of *Balkanization,* where the history can be re-imagined as congruent, through and through and syncretic, meaning being fully strategic. The criticality of the *architecture of Balkanization* lies not in its polished and disciplined history, but in its prospective, messy, improvisational: overall an *undisciplined* mix of strategy and tactics.

We have seen how the *vanishing act of socialism* in the rebuilding of an entire city like Skopje makes for the unexpected and unplanned realities, architecture and even aesthetics on the ground. A distinction has been made between a monument of urban engineering and the infrastructure from an artistic memorial commissioned by the state as a symbol of *generosity.* Late socialism in Yugoslavia can be credited with significant symbols of spatial generosity, conducted via a unique policy of *collective property.* Like the voluntary and self-organized aspects of Yugoslav *soft socialism* in building highways and dams, the return of the state can be detected in commissioning extraordinary abstract architecture for the representation of the *generous* socialist state. The two final institutional examples of withstanding the vanishing act of socialism are in Belgrade, the former capital of the former Yugoslavia: *The Museum of Aviation* and *The Yugoslav Army Headquarters.* They both remain in the possession of the former JNA (Jugoslovenska Narodna Armija), today the Army of the Republic of Serbia.

---

32 See: Thaler, Wolfgang, Vladimir Kulić, and Maroje Mrduljaš, *Modernism In-between: The Syncretic Architectures of Socialist Yugoslavia,* Berlin: Jovis Berlin, 2012.

Srdjan Jovanovic Weiss with Armin Linke

Aeronautical Museum – Belgrade Nikola Tesla Airport,
Belgrade, Serbia, Architect: Ivan Štraus, built 1989,
photographed in 2010

Belgrade's *Museum of Aviation* was founded in 1957. After a period of construction delays, the airport-adjacent building opened to the public on May 21, 1989. The expressive design of this museum is the work of Ivan Štraus, a prolific and intellectually-gifted architect from Sarajevo whose winning competition model in the shape of an acrylic green donut is still displayed at the *Museum of Aviation.* The museum's collection includes a rare model P-80, an early jet plane developed by Kelly Johnson at Lockheed Martin. The museum also displays relics of US and NATO aircraft downed during the 1990s Balkans conflicts, including wreckage from a US F-117 Nighthawk – better known as the *Stealth Bomber* – allegedly shot down using outdated Soviet radars. Paradoxically, the political system that supported the completion of this expressive building in the last days of Yugoslav Socialism later condoned the destruction of Sarajevo's built landscape, including works by the same architect.

In the bombing campaign against a rogue Serbia in 1999, NATO could not have found a more Western-style target than the Former Yugoslav Army Headquarters (also known as the Ministry of National Defense) in the downtown area of Belgrade. The site's architect Nikola Dobrović was infatuated by the Western visual theories of Henry Bergson. Bergson famously related the duration of memory and time to devise a graphic system carving into the dynamic shape of the organized matter. Dobrović took this idea of organized matter and created the building's dynamic shape to architecturally assert a Yugoslav common identity grounded in dynamism. In the press briefing by NATO the morning after its nighttime attack, this remarkable postwar modernist building was referred to as the heart of the war machine. Will this building now be remembered in relation to its creation or to its destruction? The building of the Army Headquarters coincided with the construction of the post-war national identity in Yugoslavia shortly after the break from Stalin in 1948. During the spring of 1954, the Yugoslav Army invited nine Yugoslav architects to compete for a new building complex. One of them was Nikola Dobrović, already known in leftist circles of the European intellectual avant-garde for his modernist work. Even before the competition, Theo van Doesburg, the Dutch modernist, had singled out the work of Nikola Dobrović as an architect at work in the construction of a Yugoslav national identity. Even though van Doesburg criticized Dobrović for being a true academic (not capable) in his work of formulating the constructive system of a building, the Dutch painter praised him as one of the first voices to be liberated from the limiting ties of Yugoslav tradition and to reach out toward mutual innovation in the art and architecture of Middle and Western Europe. Thus van Doesburg saw Dobrović's architecture as proof of the shift in Yugoslav politics towards a pro-liberal image endorsed by the West.[33]

Yet it is the same, though evolved, West (NATO) that reacted to the misuse of Tito's projections of a pro-liberal socialist image imbedded into the building complex of the Army Headquarters. After all, the projections last only as long as the source of projection has power. What remains is remarkable hardware, a ruin that now finally re-appears as a readable three-dimensional diagram. What started as a diagram of the future of the dynamic nation of Yugoslavia unfolds as the realizable future of its own neglect. If we continue on the anthropological line of Verdery, late socialism of Yugoslavia is finally bare-naked and finally exposed.

33 van Doesburg, Theo, "Jugoslavija: Suprostavljeni uticaji: Nikola Dobrovi i Srpska tradicija" (Yugoslavia: Conflicting Influences: Nikola Dobrovi and the Serbian Tradition) in Perovic, Milos R. and Spasoje Krunic, eds., *Nikola Dobrovi : Eseji, projekti, kritike*, Belgrade: Arhitektonski fakultet Univerziteta u Beogradu & Muzej arhitekture, 1998, 214–216.

Yugoslav Army Headquarters (today Ministry of Defense
of the Republic of Serbia), Belgrade, Serbia,
Architect: Nikola Dobrović, built 1965,
photographed in 2010

In all of these cases, the *reappearing act of socialism* enables the disappearance of the common and the equal as an axiomatic order of socialism. Under socialism, that axiom was under the umbrella of non-discrimination. Translated to the cities, infrastructure, and territory of the former Yugoslavia, this socialist axiom would not only allow but mandate equal distribution of social standards throughout the nation's federal units. That did not only mean that socialism automatically provides equal distribution of housing and infrastructure as basic necessities. It also meant that social standards reflected through education, representation, and the management of socialist history must be dispersed across a multi-ethnic socialist Yugoslavia. Large infrastructural projects like the *Highway of Brotherhood and Unity*, as well as an array of monuments, memorials, cultural facilities and museums of revolution were given priority in planning, often without clear limitations left for architects, urbanists, engineers, and artists. The limitlessness of this situation amounted to a certain autonomy of these spatial practices within the socialist system in Yugoslavia. They were to capture an emotional space of socialist Yugoslavia as a multi-ethnic effort against fascism, one that Tito kept underlying, rehearsing and repeating.[34]

This is where the split between the emotional and the sociopolitical pragmatics of spatial practices of socialist Yugoslavia start to show. The strongest resistance to socialism came not from ideological corners of the left, but from the ethnically-based pragmatics of having such a federation of indeterminate equality. Thus even the most democratic leaders in opposition to the crumbling system from the separate federal republic of Yugoslavia at the sunset of socialism were easily labelled as nationalist,

---

34 Audrey Helfant Budding's chapter in Cohen, Lenard J., and Jasna Dragović-Soso, (eds.), *State Collapse in South-Eastern Europe: New Perspectives on Yugoslavia's Disintegration*, West Lafayette, IN: Purdue UP, 2008.

moderate or extreme. This appears to be the case of the visionary Serbian leader Zoran Djindjić who opposed the Milošević abuse of emotional socialism in his own power struggles. Djindjić, who because of his reforms was assassinated in 2003, was internationally labelled as a "moderate nationalist" and was one of the first politicians to dismiss the emotional power of socialist Yugoslavia as non-pragmatic: "[Yugoslav] Federalism was unproblematic until it was expected to regulate socio-political relations. As an emotional symbol it performed its role."[35]

In short, it can be concluded that Tito's determined, pragmatic, albeit soft and indecisive stance towards ethnicity, in tandem with Edvard Kardelj as his commissar, created a nesting triangulation of strategies that affected spatial practices in the system of vanishing socialism:

1. Socialist *self-management, centripetally motivated decentralization,* the move away from the Soviet Bloc, towards softening and dismantling of the Yugoslav state. Chief architect: Edvard Kardelj; architectural production: memorials, homes of the revolution, political schools, partisan monuments, new cities, parks and recreation;

2. Ethnically and nationalistically driven *collectivism,* being more occupied with territorial issues than urban issues, carving out overlapped ethnic and nationalistic space, not as the space of inhabitation, but the territory of emotional, and criminal discharge. Chief architects: Slobodan Milošević, Franjo Tudjman, Alija Izetbegović; collateral architectural production: *illegal architecture, Turbo architecture,* camps, enclaves, slums.

---

35 Đinđić, Zoran, Jugoslavija kao nedovršena država, 28. Cf. Slobodan Samardžić, "Federalizm u Švajcarskoj i Jugoslaviji – ustavni koncepti u političke institucije," in Thomas Flajner and Slobodan Samardžić (eds.), *Federalizam i problem manjina u višeetničkim zajednicama - uporedna analiza Švajcarske i Jugoslavije,* Belgrade: Institut za evropske studije, 1995), 95–98.

3. *Third way.* Non-aligned spatial practices: un-ideological, global and share-based initiatives for better life. Chief architects: Josip Broz Tito, Nehru, Nasser. Architectural production: activism, reclamation of privatized collective land, international practice, transfer of socialist engineering, research practice, participatory urbanism.

We need to take the architecture of Balkanization into analysis as a driving force in the making of contemporary territory of Yugoslavia. Today, in the emerging fragments out of Yugoslavia, the vanishing ideology of socialism reappears as new spatial culture. This culture reappears under the auspices of distinct nation states, often with overlaps. At the same time, the process of Balkanization has shown that it can fuel the production of distinct spaces as never before. The production of capital cities in former Yugoslavia, from having one until 1991 to having seven in 2012, radically alters practices as self-styled cultures of distinction via spatial practice. Due to Balkanization, these new capital cities now look elsewhere again in search of exceptionalism. Kardelj's call for decentralization during late socialism became reality. Each young capital coming out of Yugoslavia demonstrates how to craft its own distinct image among the rest in the group of seven in the region. That is a positive aspect of Balkanization. This is because each of the seven capital cities are crafting different ways of being distinct. Yet, the vanishing act of socialism – solidified in this architecture – reappears today in unexpected and informal ways. What are those ways? The success of Yugoslav architecture is seen as the future from the past, as symbols of a new archipelago of common life. This new life of architecture from socialism out of Yugoslavia is today practiced in a decentralized manner among its new nation states. Kardelj might have loved this. Why? Because as we have seen, the ideological system of Yugoslavia was dismantled only to pass on its symbols in architecture to every new nation by itself. That in itself can be looked at as a positive aspect of Balkanization. Again why? Because the seed of architecture of socialism is not lost. It has been decentralized, and is now reappearing as an archipelago of monuments throughout contemporary Yugoslavia. As their ideological public vanished with socialist demise, these monuments and institutions are today more accessible than they were ever intended to be.

Acknowledgments

Srdjan Jovanovic Weiss and Armin Linke would like to thank:

Abitare Magazine, Centre for Research Architecture Goldsmiths, Codex, CZKD Belgrade, ETH Zürich, Fall Semester Miami, Graham Foundation, HDLU Zagreb, JRP RIngier Zürich, Museum of Yugoslav History Belgrade, Storefront for Art and Architecture New York, kuda.org – New Media Center Novi Sad, Mama & Platforma 9.81 Zagreb & School of Missing Studies.

And: Ellen Hartwell Alderman, Tobia Bezzola, Stefano Boeri, Markus Bosshard, Lindsay Bremner, Gavin Browning, Giulia Bruno, Eric Bunge, Alfredo Brillenburg, Eduardo Cadava, Katherine Carl, Jean-Louis Cohen, Teddy Cruz, Goran Djordjević, Helena Drnovšek, Zenit Đozić, Eva Franch i Gilabert, Homa Farjadi, Annette Fierro, Branko Franceschi, Pedro Gadanho, Fabrizio Gallanti, Joseph Grimma, Richard Gluckman, Sarah Herda, Manuel Hertz, Mimi Hoang, Ana Janevski, Ružica and Miodrag Jovanović, Filip Jovanovski, Anna Katz, Edvard Kardelj, Veselinka Kastratović, Ivan Kucina, Vladimir Kulić, Ivan and Maja Lalić, Aaron Levi, Anja Lutz, Ana Miljački, Marcel Mars, Reinhold Martin, William Menking, Miodrag Mitrašinović, Maroje Mrduljaš, Academic Marko Mušič, Sina Najafi, Minna Ninova, Vladimir Lalo Nikolić, John Palmesino, Borka Pavićević, Antonio Petrov, James Pike, Haris Piplas, Philip Plowright, Sarah Poppel, Marjetica Potrč, Nikola Radić Lucati, Nina Rappaport, Snežana Ristić, Irit Rogoff, Ann-Sofi Rönnskog, Jenny Sabin, Yehuda Safran, Marko Sančanin, Scott Schall, Ena Schulz, Susan Schuppli, Florian Schneider, Karl Seitz, Dubravka Sekulić, Lidija Slavković, Martino Stierli, Branimir Stojanović, Alenka Suhadolnik, Jürg Trösch, Josip Broz Tito, Milica Tomić, Ksenija Turčić, Philip Ursprung, Katarina Živanović, Odalis Valdivieso,

Acknowledgments

Bostjan Vuga, Lea Vene, Borislav Vukićević, Eyal Weizman, Ines Weizman, Ivana Wingham and Mark Wigley.
and to everyone helping, hosting, driving us around and being so generous.

Thank you.

This book is dedicated to Katherine and Julian

Supported by Graham Foundation for Advanced Studies in the Fine Arts, Chicago

Graham Foundation

This content is partly adapted from a doctoral thesis: "Architecture of Balkanization" by Srdjan Jovanovic Weiss defended at the Centre for Research Architecture, Department of Visual Cultures, Goldsmiths University of London in 2013

Note:
This publication follows an earlier book, "Socialist Architecture: The Vanishing Act" by Armin Linke and Srdjan Jovanovic Weiss, published by JRP Ringier, Zürich in 2012.

Socialist Architecture – The Reappearing Act
by Srdjan Jovanovic Weiss
with a series of photographs by Armin Linke

Text partially edited by: Gavin Browning, Minna Ninova
and Katherine Carl
Proofreading: Robert Schlicht
Layout: Anja Lutz // Book Design, Corinna Northe
Image processing: Hausstaetter Herstellung, Berlin
Print production: Standartu Spaustuve, Lithuania

ISBN 978-3-941644-92-2

Published by

THE
GREENBOX

The Green Box
Kunst Editionen, Berlin
www.thegreenbox.net